A look at ALCOHOLISM

Lerner Awareness Series

A look at ALCOHOLISM

photographs by Maria S. Forrai

text by Rebecca Anders

foreword by Henry Winkler

Minneapolis

The publisher wishes to thank Carleton College, the Hennepin County Detoxification Center, On-Top, Richard's Bar, and the St. Kevin School for their cooperation in the preparation of this book.

In taking the pictures for this book, the photographer used a 2¼" x 2¼" single-lens reflex Bronica. The film used was Kodak Tri-X-Pan, and the pictures were printed on Ilfospeed photographic paper. The text of the book is set in 14 point Baskerville, and the book paper is 80# Black-and-White Gloss enamel.

LIBRARY OF CONGRESS CATALOGING IN PUBLICATION DATA

Forrai, Maria S.
A look at alcoholism.

(Lerner Awareness Series)
SUMMARY: Text and photographs describe the problems of alcohol abuse.

1. Alcoholism—Pictorial works—Juvenile literature. [1. Alcoholism] I. Anders, Rebecca. II. Title.

HV5066.F67 1978 362.2'92 77-12981
ISBN 0-8225-1311-0

Published simultaneously in Canada by J. M. Dent & Sons (Canada) Ltd., Don Mills, Ontario. Manufactured in the United States of America.

International Standard Book Number: 0-8225-1311-0
Library of Congress Catalog Card Number: 77-12981

3 4 5 6 7 8 9 10 85 84 83 82 81

Henry Winkler talks about Alcoholism . . .

It's wonderful to be alive! We can do anything that we can imagine, as long as our imaginations are clear. One of our most important jobs while we're growing is to take good care of ourselves, our minds as well as our bodies. We have a choice. We can fill our minds with good thoughts that become building blocks on which to build our lives. Or we can hurt our minds, thereby hurting our lives.

Have you ever thought of being a doctor, an actor, an astronaut? You can do it, but drinking alcohol will stop you in your tracks. Your dreams will never take shape if your mind isn't working right.

Love yourself. Take care of yourself. Stand up for yourself. Be cool.

Cool is never having to do what a friend does, just to be part of the group.

I love you,

Henry Winkler

Alcohol is a strong drug that affects people's minds and bodies. For centuries, it has been a part of human life. In the past, many societies used wine in their religious ceremonies. Even today, alcohol has an important place in special ceremonies and celebrations. And down through the ages, alcoholic drinks have been used in everyday life.

In our society, people drink on many different occasions. Some families drink wine or beer with their meals. Alcohol is often served at parties, when friends meet to have a good time. On these occasions, people get together to eat and talk and enjoy each other's company. Drinking plays only a small part in their enjoyment.

People use alcohol in other ways. Some people feel that they must drink in order to have a good time. Or they feel that they need alcohol to relax. Others can't face their jobs or their daily lives without a drink or two. When people come to depend on alcohol in these ways, they may have a drinking problem.

Alcoholics are people with very serious drinking problems. For them, alcohol is the most important thing in the world. Drinking is no longer something they choose to do. It is something they *must* do. Their bodies have become dependent on a powerful drug, and they suffer without it.

Alcoholics are sick people. The desire for alcohol controls their lives.

Alcoholics often have trouble keeping their jobs. Because alcohol slows down the brain, a worker who has been drinking may make mistakes on the job. These mistakes can be both expensive and dangerous. Problem drinkers may sometimes feel so sick that they will not be able to come to work at all.

People who drink too much can do permanent damage to their bodies. Too much alcohol taken over a long period of time can injure the liver, the kidneys, and even the brain. Because people who are drinking heavily do not have control over their movements, they may also hurt themselves in falls and accidents.

THE SECRET

Problem drinkers not only hurt themselves, but they also hurt others. More than half of all injuries and deaths on the highways involve people who have been drinking.

Because alcoholics are sick people, they need the help of doctors and other specialists. They can often get this help at hospitals and "detoxification" centers. At these places, alcoholics can obtain aid for their medical problems. They can also find out about ways in which they can begin to help themselves.

Alcoholism is a serious problem in modern society. In the United States, it is the third largest health problem, after heart disease and cancer. The cost of alcoholism to the country, including lost work time, may be as high as $15 billion each year. The disease of alcoholism is so common that nearly everyone is affected by it in some way.

The pain and unhappiness caused by alcoholism creates special problems in families. When one member of the family is an alcoholic, all the other family members are affected. Alcoholism is particularly hard on young people.

BOODLES
BRITISH
GIN

When a parent has a drinking problem, he or she may not be able to give the children in the family what they need. The family's money may be used to buy alcohol instead of food and clothes. The children may be left on their own while Mom and Dad spend their time drinking. Children may even be physically hurt if alcohol makes their parents violent.

Sometimes a parent's drinking problem is passed on to the children in the family. Children may follow Mom's or Dad's example and begin drinking at home. They may learn to depend on alcohol at an early age. What many young people do not know is that their growing bodies can be permanently injured by the early use of alcohol.

MOGEN DAVID

When young people come to depend on alcohol, they have the same kinds of problems that adults have. Their health suffers. They have trouble keeping up with normal activities. They may even drop out of school or lose their jobs.

ACE

People with drinking problems may feel so confused and unhappy that they think no one can help. But help *can* be found. The first step in controlling alcoholism is to understand the problem and to reach out for aid.

Teachers or counselors at school can help young people who have drinking problems or whose parents drink too much. City and state officials can also help. And there are special organizations and groups just for people with this kind of problem.

Alcoholism is an illness, but it is not a hopeless one. Alcoholics can get better, with hard work and the help of many people.

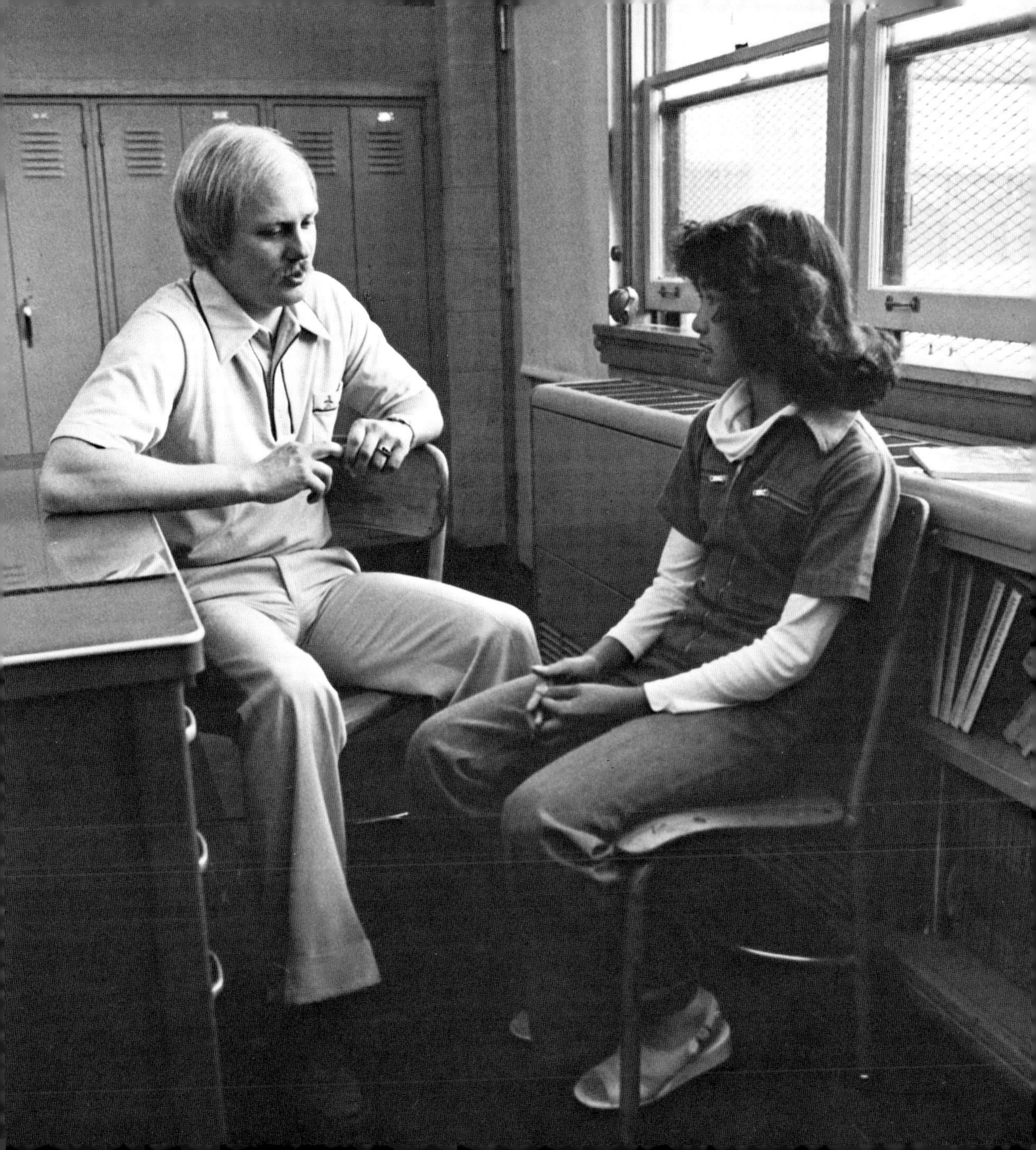

About the Artist

Maria S. Forrai makes her living by taking photographs. "Photography is a family tradition with me," she explains. "In Hungary, where I was born, my mother became a very good portrait photographer. And here in the United States, my husband and I are establishing ourselves as architectural photographers. Designers and builders hire us to take dramatic pictures of their schools, shopping centers, and office buildings." In addition to the work she does with her husband, Maria likes to photograph people. "I try to show the reality of people's lives in my photographs," says Maria. "I want to capture what they are thinking and feeling."

Many of Maria's photographs have won prizes. They have been on display in Leipzig, Germany, as well as in Budapest, Hungary. More recently, her work has been shown at the University of Illinois and at the University of Minnesota. Maria lives with her husband and two children in St. Paul, Minnesota.